THE LATIN VERSIONS

OF

JUDITH

BY

EDWIN EDGAR VOIGT

A DISSERTATION
Presented to the Faculty of the Graduate School
of Yale University in candidacy for the
Degree of Doctor of Philosophy

WIPF & STOCK · Eugene, Oregon

Wipf and Stock Publishers
199 W 8th Ave, Suite 3
Eugene, OR 97401

The Latin Versions of Judith
By Voigt, Edwin Edgar
Softcover ISBN-13: 978-1-6667-6334-8
Hardcover ISBN-13: 978-1-6667-6335-5
eBook ISBN-13: 978-1-6667-6336-2
Publication date 10/28/2022
Previously published by Offizin W. Drugulin, 1925

This edition is a scanned facsimile of the original edition published in 1925.

TABLE OF CONTENTS

	Page
Foreword	5
Introduction	7
I. The Greek Versions	9
II. The Old Latin	13
Regius 3564 and Sangermanensis 4	14
Sangermanensis 15	20
Pechianus	29
Corbeiensis 7	35
Summary of the Old Latin	44
III. The Vulgate	46
Bibliography	55

FOREWORD

At the outset this study was undertaken with the end in view of reaching a better understanding of the family relationships of the Old Testament manuscripts. But in a short time it became apparent that probably the distinctive thing which the Book of Judith might teach, especially from a textual point of view, had to do with the Latin manuscripts, for here are found a number of versions that do not otherwise stand side by side. Consequently, it has seemed of sufficient importance to avoid a general discussion of the versions and confine this one to the sources and relationships of the Latin.

To Professor Charles Cutler Torrey, under whose direction this study was made, and whose kindly counsel and valuable suggestions have been an inestimable aid, I wish to extend my sincerest gratitude.

INTRODUCTION

The book of Judith of the Old Testament Apocrypha exists in the Greek, Latin and Syriac versions. That none of these is the original, and that the original was Hebrew, has long been recognized by writers in the field. Only a Semitic writer would use, for example, the preposition "in" to express agent, or pray "toward the face of the temple," or slay "with the mouth of the sword," or "give a great voice." Such Hebrew idioms are so numerous throughout the Greek and Latin, and are so baldly translated, that it seems altogether unnecessary to go into a further discussion of the original language of the book.

Origen's statement (Ep. ad Afr.), "Ἑβραῖοι τῷ Τωβία οὐ χρῶνται, οὐδὲ τῇ Ἰουδήθ· οὐδὲ γὰρ ἔχουσιν αὐτὰ καὶ ἐν ἀποκρύφοις ἑβραιστί, ὡς ἀπ' αὐτῶν μαθόντες ἐγνώκαμεν," shows that the Hebrew version must have perished not later than the early part of the second century. Subsequently the transmission of the text depended upon versions in languages other than the original. The oldest of these and, as we shall see, the one unquestionably nearest the original is the Greek.

As for the Latin, Judith is found in five manuscripts of the "Old Latin" Version, as well as in St. Jerome's Vulgate. Better opportunity for studying the Old Latin probably does not exist than in the Book of Judith, for these five Old Latin Mss. nowhere else stand side by side. Consequently, we have here an exceptional opportunity of coming into a better understanding of the character of this version; and the evaluation of these manuscripts will occupy the main portion of the following discussion, in the course of which the dependence of the Old Latin upon the Greek and the impossibility of longer using the term "Old Latin" as embracing a single recension will appear, we trust, with sufficient clearness.

St. Jerome's Vulgate, on the other hand, probably has not the relation to the Old Latin that some of the past commentators have supposed. It is indeed doubtful whether the Vulgate was influenced by the Old Latin at all; rather, it is a translation of an Aramaic version, which in the absence of the Hebrew was translated from some Greek version for the use of the Jews in later years. Indeed, Saint Jerome says in his preface that he made his translation from a "Chaldee" version, and in the following pages, it is hoped, more light can be thrown on the reliability of his statements.

Finally, consideration of the Syriac version will hardly come within the scope of this inquiry. On the one hand because of its lateness it certainly could not have influenced the Old Latin, while on the other the peculiar circumstances connecting the Vulgate with an Aramaic recension indicate that the Syriac version has no bearing here.

The variant readings of the Old Latin and of the Vulgate, which will be pointed out in the following pages, have been taken from the compilation of D. Petrus Sabatier, *Biblorum Sacrorum Latinae Versiones Antiquae*. This work of Sabatier is the only satisfactory effort in existence in which the Old Latin versions have been compiled, and for nearly two-hundred years scholars and students not having access to the actual manuscripts have found this compilation a very valuable source book. For the variants in the Greek manuscripts we are indebted to Holmes and Parsons, *Vetus Testamentum Graecum*, compared with H. B. Swete's *Old Testament in Greek*. The work of Holmes and Parsons likewise has been found to be very reliable, and comparison with Swete would have been unnecessary but for the fact that the latter gives the variant readings of Codex Aleph, which of course was unknown in Holmes and Parsons time.

I
THE GREEK VERSIONS

On account of the fact that the Greek is fundamental to this investigation, it is of first importance to have an accurate idea of the relation existing among the various Greek Manuscripts, of which a goodly number preserve the book of Judith. The Greek Mss. in which Judith is found are the great uncial codices A, B, and Aleph, and the cursive Mss., about twenty in number, assembled in Holmes and Parsons, in which list 23 is in reality an uncial, also known as Codex N, of Venice.

The three uncial codices stand in fairly close agreement, particularly in the more important readings. Among the three Aleph has more variants than either of the others. Codex B differs from A and Aleph in at least eighty instances; A varies from the other two not less than one hundred times; while Aleph reads alone more than one hundred and fifty times. By far the majority of these variations are of minor importance and of a negligible character as far as this study is concerned, since for the most part they involve the addition or omission of a copulative word, differences in the use of pronouns, variations in case endings, and lack of agreement of the number in verbs. To illustrate, Codex A reads καθα for καθαρα in 12:9, and in 6:4, ὅρα for ὅρια. In 16:2, Codex B has καὶ αἶνον for καίνον. In 1:2, B reads ἐν τῇ Μωάβ where the others read ἐν γῇ Μωάβ— —a confusion easy to make in uncial characters where the letters T and Γ are easily interchanged and TH can readily be read for ΓΗ, or vice versa. At various times all add or omit αὐτοῦ, αὐτῆς, or αὐτῶν. Such variations, of course, are nothing other than carelessness in copying, and, in this carelessness Aleph seems to have been the worst offender especially since it is prone to omit phrases and even clauses. However, the material thus omitted is not of a significant nature, and the omissions may be the result of a conscious effort on the part of the scribe to abbreviate (see also, 6:10; 9:7; 10:3; 13:14; 15:3; 16:24, &c.).

On the other hand, there are some variants that can not be ascribed to the causes enumerated above. For instances, when A reads ἐπαρχίαν for παραλίαν (3:6), or ἀπάτησιν for ἀπάντησιν (10:4), it is more than a question of carelessness or stupidity, and seems to be a conscious effort to improve the text. Likewise, the readings of B, ἐκέλευσεν for πρόσταξεν (2:15), and βοήθειαν for βοηθῆσαι (Aleph reads βληθεῖν), are to be preferred above the rest. On the other hand, when A reads γένους for ἔθνους (12:3), or κλῆσιν for χρῆσιν (12:10), and Aleph has χρήματα for ἅρματα (1:14), these readings are inferior to the others. Again, in the instance in 16:4 when A reads ἀνελεῖν ἐν ῥομφαίᾳ, while the others omit the preposition, it more literally reproduces the Hebrew idiom, for the Hebrew would certainly have used the preposition "Beth." However, ἐν may accidentally have dropped out of the other Greek Mss. Once more, in 2:25 Aleph reads οὐκ ἔστι βοηθῶν ἡμῖν, and the rest, οὐκ ἔστι βοηθὸς ἡμῶν, in which case Aleph probably is nearest the Hebrew, אֵין עֹזֵר לָנוּ.

Meanwhile, mention should also be made here of the relations of the uncial codices to the cursive manuscripts. The cursives fall into four groups, which of course show some indication of mutual contamination, but which nevertheless have very characteristic family peculiarities: (1) Ms. 58 (according to the numeration in Holmes and Parsons), (2) Mss. 19 and 108, (3) Mss. 44, 71, 74, 76, 106, 107, 236, and (4) Mss. 51, 52, 64, 243, 248, 249, Comp., Ald., Alex., while Mss. 23 and 55 are hard to identify with any group. The 4th Group, although not consistently aligned with codex A and obviously compared with other textual traditions and corrupted by scribal errors, still attests the tradition of A to a much larger extent than any other. The 3rd Group is probably somewhat closer related to Codex B. Codex Aleph appears to have been parent of none of the cursives, although its variants are sometimes found in all the cursive groups. The variants of Aleph rarely appear in the A-group; they appear in the B-group in some thirty instances, in 19 and 108 about forty times, and in 58 about fifty times. The seeming large number of agreements with 19 and 108 and with 58 are in reality only a very small portion of their total variations; so the Aleph-tradition appears not to have been widely disseminated.

Ms. 58, however, for our study is by far the most interesting manuscript in the collection, uncials included. In more than five hundred instances does it vary from the uncial codices, and there is hardly a verse in the book in which it does not show some individual peculiarity. It differs in every way in which it is possible for a manuscript to differ, changes of construction, new words, omissions, inversions, and even transposition of clauses are of common occurrence. It is a most interesting question, why this manuscript should be so different from the rest. Why would a scribe, for instance, make such unnecessary word changes as, $\pi\alpha\iota\delta\acute{o}s$ for $\delta o\acute{v}\lambda o\upsilon$ (5:5), $\theta\upsilon\gamma\alpha\tau\acute{e}\rho\alpha s$ for $\tau\acute{e}\kappa\nu\alpha$ (7:27), $\theta\rho\acute{e}\mu\mu\alpha$ for $\pi\rho\acute{o}\beta\alpha\tau\alpha$ (8:26), $\pi o\rho\epsilon\acute{v}\epsilon\sigma\theta\alpha\iota$ for $\grave{e}\xi\epsilon\lambda\epsilon\acute{v}\epsilon\sigma\theta\alpha\iota$ (13:3) or $\mu\epsilon\tau\grave{\alpha}$ $\mu\iota\kappa\rho\acute{o}\nu$ for $\mu\epsilon\tau'$ $\grave{o}\lambda\acute{\iota}\gamma o\nu$ (13:9)? Or again, why would he write "the family of the sons of Israel" for "the family of Israel" (6:2)? In 16:16, where the uncials tell us that the "elders and young men and women gathered for the assembly," why would Ms. 58 write "the elders and young men and their children, &c.," or why would it have "upon the turrets of their walls" for "upon their walls" (7:5), or "the two together went out and went to the gate" instead of "they went out to the gate" (10:6)?

In each instance the differences are noteworthy, for they clearly show that 58 came from a tradition altogether different from the one back of the rest of the Greek. If in the end 58 came from the same parent from which the rest of the Greek Mss. came, such differences (which are typical and can be multiplied many times) would reveal habits of copying that would be new in the history of the transmission of manuscripts, for no scribe would make the word changes or the additions that have been pointed out without more authority than we have before us, and the only conclusion possible is that this manuscript, or its ultimate ancestor, came from an altogether different recension. Now, as to these changes and additions (or ommissions which are just as common), are they not precisely the differences one might find in an oral account? Judith certainly was a tale that was told and retold many times, and doubtlessly in some sections transmitted by word of mouth, an exercise which would be no great feat for an oriental, and it seems very reasonable to suppose that some narrator, whose story was finally put into writing, could be expected to produce just such a recension with just such variations as we have in Ms. 58.

There remain, finally, the two cursive manuscripts 19 and 108. These have about 150 variations from the other Greek Mss. In about half of these instances the reading is the same as in Ms. 58, and it is not uncommon for many of the rest of the cursives to attest these readings. But in come notable instances 19 and 108 read alone; e. g., in 6:4 they read τοῦ στόματος for τῶν λόγον, a reading which two of the Old Latin Mss. attest, and in 12:18 they have ψυχή for ζῆν, which is attested by the other three Old Latin Mss.

In 11:9, to the phrase πάντα ὅσα ἐξελάλησε they add πάντας τοὺς λόγους σου, apparently a phrase designed further to explain πάντα. In 7:20 for τριάκοντα τέσσαρες they read δέκα τέσσαρες καὶ μῆνα ἕνα, possibly an instance when the scribe misread the uncial abbreviations for thirty-four, ΛΔ, as fourteen, ΙΔ, and then knowing that the cisterns would not dry up in so short a time hazarded the guess, "a month and fourteen days;" at least, that there was some doubt about this reading is attested by the fact that one of the Old Latin manuscripts (Sang. 15) reads, "quatuor et mensibus duobus."

However, for the most part Mss. 19 and 108 show that their variants, when they are unattested, are the result of misreading what was before them, and in other cases the result of an effort to clarify the meaning of the text. The fact, as already mentioned, that they frequently read with Ms. 58 indicates, also, that some time in their history they were affected by the 58-recension.

II
THE OLD LATIN

The Book of Judith is preserved in five Old Latin manuscripts, Regius 3564, Sangermanensis 4, Sangermanensis 15, Corbeiensis 7, and Pechianus. In general the first thing to be noted is that the Old Latin is taken from the Greek rather than from the Hebrew. For the occurrence of certain mistranslations must be explained with reference to the Greek rather than the Hebrew. When the Greek narrates about Judith's personal servant, the word commonly used is ἄβρα; the Old Latin frequently translates this word as, "abra," a word unknown to the Latin (cf. 10:2, 14. 8:10). Likewise, in the Old Latin one finds the proper name "Prionem" (3:9, 4:6), where the Greek reads τοῦ πριονός, a term which the Latin translator failed to understand, and therefore transliterated. So too, "cidarim" (or "cidares") for κιδάρεις (4:5). Such mistakes present very strong evidence that the Old Latin was a translation from the Greek rather than from the Hebrew, for such readings, and especially the first two, indubitably show the Greek influence.

Furthermore, ever since Fritzsche's studies in Judith in 1853 it has commonly been the judgment of writers that the Old Latin was dependent upon Ms. 58, with Mss. 19 and 108 in some measure affiliated. It is indeed clear after even a hasty survey that the peculiarities of 58 have somehow found their way into the Old Latin, as a few instances out of a large number will show:

4:6. Uncials et al. ἥ ἐστιν ἀπέναντι Ἐσδρηλών
     Ms. 58,   ἥ ἐστιν ἐπάνω τοῦ πριονός ἀπέναντι Ἐσδρηλών
     Regius,   quae est super Prionem contra Esdrelon

4:6. Sangerman. 4, quae est contra Priornis contra Esdrelon
Sangerman. 15, quae est contra Prionem contra Esdrelon
Corbeiensis, quae est contra Prionem contra Esdrelon

2:21. Uncials et al. πλησίον τοῦ ὄρους τοῦ ἐπὶ ἀριστερᾷ
Ms. 58, πλησίον τοῦ ὄρους τοῦ ἀγγίου οὗ ἐστιν ἐπὶ ἀριστερᾷ
Reg. Sang. 4, justa montem Agga qui est in sinistra
Sang. 15, justa montem Ageant qui est in sinistra
Corbeiensis, justa montem ange qui est in sinistra

The occurrence of Prionem (and variants) and of Agga (although ἀγγίου is apparently a corruption of ἄνω) in these two passages clearly shows the relation of the Old Latin to the Greek of Ms. 58; for since these two words are found only in 58, and since the Latin could not have been taken from the Hebrew, as pointed out above, illustrations such as these make it clear why it has generally been held that the Old Latin was allied to the recension represented in Ms. 58.

However, the difficulty with saying that Old Latin and Ms. 58 read together lies in the fact that the term "Old Latin" is made to include too much. Such use of the term "Old Latin" should mean that the Old Latin Mss. go back to a single ancestor, and that the variants among them are merely the results of mistakes in copying. But as we study the Mss. individually, there seems to be a greater divergence among them than this [1], and as a result the customary use of the term "Old Latin" will have to be abandoned for being too loose in meaning, and it will no longer be sufficient to say, merely, that the Old Latin reads with Ms. 58, but it will be necessary to designate individual manuscripts of the Old Latin.

REGIUS 3564 AND SANGERMANENSIS 4

The text which Sabatier places opposite the Vulgate as the most characteristic Old Latin text is that found in these two manuscripts. As compared to the text of the Greek uncial

---

[1] Cf. below, pp. 20 ff., 29 ff., 38 ff.

codices it is very complete, having preserved practically the same amount of the book; what additions or omissions there are, being without importance to the trend of the narrative. There are less than a dozen instances in the entire book in which these two Old Latin manuscripts fail to agree, and the variants that do occur are limited almost entirely to single words. To illustrate, in 7:11 for πρός Reg. reads "adversus" and Sang. 4 reads "ad;" in 4:6 for ἐπάνω Reg. writes "super" and Sang. 4, "contra;" in 8:10 for ἄβραν Reg. has "ancilla" and Sang. 4, "abram;" in 11:4 for κάθα γίνεται Reg. has "sicut feci" and Sang 4, "sicut sit;" and in 10:21 for καθυφασμένων Reg. has "contextum" while Sang. 4 has "justa eum." Some of these illustrations, particularly "abram" and "justa eum," rather seem to show that Sang. 4 is the less reliable of the two; however, on so few instances of minor importance the relative merits of two manuscripts can hardly be judged. Sabatier writes in his preface to Judith that Regius comes from about the year 900, and that Sangermanensis 4 is "eiusdem aetatis." Consequently, it is very probable that they are copies of the same parent manuscript. In the following pages, accordingly, they will be dealt with as representing a single text.

In examining them one cannot go far without seeing that they were not translated from the Greek text which have in the uncial codices, but that they resemble more closely the text of Ms. 58; to illustrate.

4:13. Uncials, κατὰ πρόσωπον τῶν ἁγίων Κυρίου παντοκράτορος
Ms. 58, καὶ ἔπεσον κατὰ πρόσωπον τῶν ἡγιασμένων Κυρίου παντοκράτορος
Reg. Sang. 4, et prociderunt contra faciem sanctorum Domini omnipotentis

13:4. Uncials, κατελείφθη ἐν τῷ κοιτῶνι ἀπὸ μικροῦ ἕως μεγάλου
Ms. 58, ὑπελείφθη ἐν τῷ κοιτῶνι αὐτοῦ μικρὸς ἢ μέγας
Reg. Sang. 4, relictus est in cubiculo eius magnus vel pusillus

In both of these instances one sees an obvious resemblance between the text of Ms. 58 and that of Reg. and Sang. 4, and in such cases it seems to be true that these Old Latin Mss. did not use the uncial text.

In a similar manner there are many places where Ms. 58 has added to the uncial text, and Reg. and Sang. 4 follow the same reading. In 13:10, Ms. 58 reads πᾶσαν τὴν φάραγγα where the rest of the Greek has τὴν φάραγγα, and Reg. and Sang. 4 attest the reading of 58 by having "totam vallem," whereas Corbeiensis, the only other Old Latin Ms. having the phrase, reads with the uncial text, "vallem." Again, in 5:15, Ms. 58 adds the words καὶ Βασινιτάς, and Reg. and Sang. 4. alone attest the reading with the words, "et Basanites."

Further, frequently when Ms. 58 makes an omission, these two Old Latin Mss. make the same omission; e. g.,

2:28. Uncials,   καὶ οἱ κατοικοῦντας ἐν Ἀζώτῳ
Ms. 58,   καὶ   ἐν Ἀζώτῳ
Reg. Sang. 4,   et   Azoto
Sang. 15,   et omnes qui erant in Azotum
Corbeiensis   et inhabitantes in Azoto

The relation between Reg. and Sang. 4 and Ms. 58, in that all omit οἱ κατοικοῦντας, is again very obvious. The fact that the other Old Latin Mss. attest this phrase shows that the reading of Reg. and Sang. 4 could not have been suggested by a Latin source.

7:10, Uncials,   ἐν τοῖς αὐτοὶ ἐνοικοῦσιν ἐν αὐτοῖς
Ms. 58,   ἐν τοῖς αὐτοὶ ἐνοικοῦσιν
Reg. Sang. 4,   in quibus habitant
Sang. 15,   in quibus inhabitant in ipsis

In this instance 58 seems to have attempted to correct a very common Hebrew idiom, which the uncial text rendered literally, and Reg. and Sang. 4 have followed that correction, whereas, Sang. 15 has given us a bit of Latin as Hebraistic as the Greek of the Uncial text.

8:26, Uncials,   μετὰ Ἀβραὰμ καὶ ὅσα
                  ἐπείρασε   τὸν Ἰσαάκ
Ms. 58,   μετὰ Ἀβραὰμ   καὶ Ἰσαάκ

8:26, Reg. Sang. 4,　cum Abraham　　　et Isaac
Sang. 15, Pech.,　cum Abraham　　　et cum Isaac
Corbeiensis,　　Abrahae quemadmodum
　　　　　　　　tentaverunt　　　eum et Isaac

Here Reg. and Sang. 4 follow the reading of 58 perfectly, but Sang. 15 supplied a second "cum," although its reading obviously came from the same source also, which could not have been the text of the uncial codices. Corb., however, keeping the longer reading, indicates its independence of Ms. 58.

Then too, Ms. 58 has made many word changes, in which Reg. and Sang. 4 concur; e. g., in 10:4 for the word ἀπάτησιν Ms. 58 reads ἁρπαγήν, and Reg. and Sang. 4 have "rapinam," while Sang. 15 (the only other V. L. Ms. to have the phrase) reads, "abalienationem." Again, in 16:21 Ms. 58 reads σκηνώματα where the rest of the Greek has κληρονομίαν, and Reg. and Sang. 4, following the reading of 58, have "tabernacula," but the rest of the V. L. Mss. have "possessionem," a closer translation of the Greek of the uncials. Once more, in 11:19 Ms. 58 reads ἐμηνύθη for ἐλαλήθη, to which Reg. and Sang. 4 alone attest, reading "ostensa sunt," while the others read with the uncial Greek, "dicta sunt."

Consequently, since these instances are only part of the list that could be brought forward, it is certain that there was more than an accidental relationship between Reg. and Sang. 4 and Ms. 58. It is not possible, however, to say that they belong to the same recension, for there are a great many readings of Ms. 58 that these two Old Latin manuscripts do not attest,[1] and as a result it does not seem likely that more can be said than that some time in the history of the recension represented by Reg. and Sang. 4 it was contaminated by a manuscript belonging to the same recension as Ms. 58, rather than that the contamination was made by 58 itself.

Another fact to be noted about Reg. and Sang. 4 is that they are prone to make free translations of the Greek and to use circumlocutions of expression. That they had access

---

[1] Cf. below, pp. 20 ff.

to a text otherwise unknown seems unlikely, for they did not especially alter the meaning, but in many cases they seem to render the meaning rather than translate the words. The following instances will show their habits in this respect:

2:11, Greek, ἐπὶ δὲ τοὺς ἀπειθοῦντες
Reg. Sang. 4, super eos qui non obediunt
Other V. L., super contemnentes autem

The freedom of Reg. and Sang. 4 in rendering the participle is noteworthy, and yet it seems more than likely that they are depending on the same Greek as we have here.

16:25, Greek, ὁ ἐκφοβῶν
Reg. Sang. 4, qui in timore mitteret
Other V. L., qui perturbaret

Here again, as above, Reg. and Sang. 4 give the equivalent of the Greek, although not the literal equivalent.

14:13, Greek, ἵνα ἐξολοθρευθῶσαν εἰς τέλος
Reg. Sang. 4, ut pereant usque in finem
Other V. L., ut exterminentur in consummationem
(Corb. exterminent)

In this case the freedom of translation of Reg. and Sang. 4 seems to be in the interest of more idiomatic Latin, and their version is not as Hebraistic as that in the other Old Latin manuscripts.

14:9, Greek, ὡς δὲ ἐπαύσατο λαλοῦσα
Reg. Sang. 4, et postquam desiit loqui
Corbeiensis, quae cum cessasset loquendo
Sang. 15, quae cum cessasset ("Loquendo" probably dropped out)

Although "desiit loqui" might stand as a translation of the Greek, yet it shows one of the dominant characteristic of these two Mss,, namely their independence of the Old Latin.

Moreover, there are instances where the freedom and independence of Reg. and Sang. 4 seems to have lead them to make an attempt to clarify the meaning of the text by additions of their own; e. g., in 14:11 where the narrative relates what was done with the head of Olofernes, the Greek reads, ἐκρέμασαν ... ἐκ τοῦ τείχους, and Reg. and Sang. 4 specify the actions of the people a little more clearly by writing, "subierunt et suspenderunt... in muro." In 6:21 where the Greek reads, παρέλαβεν ... εἰς οἶκον αὐτοῦ, they clarify the Greek by reading, "eduxit... et duxit illam in domum." Likewise in 8:23, they strengthen the reading of the Greek, εἰς ἀτιμίαν, by having, "sine honore in depraedationem."

These instances show both the independence of Reg. and Sang. 4 from the rest of the Old Latin, and also the freedom with which they translated what seems likely to have been the same Greek as still exists. So it seems that they came from an age when the translator did not have a fanatical reverence for the text, and was willing to make his translation in a free and easy way, unimcumbered with a feeling and desire for literal accuracy.

Finally, reference might be made to the instances, really few in number, in which Reg. and Sang. 4 seem to have been guilty of error. E. g., in 6:3 their translation of τὸ κράτος τῶν ἵππων is "spumam equorum." In 1:2 they make the height of the wall 60 cubits, the Greek having 70 cubits. Here they might have got this reading by mistake from 1:4, where, like Codex Aleph, they make the height of the gates 60 cubits. Again, in 7:25, for the expression, ἐν δίψῃ καὶ ἀπολείᾳ, they read "siti in perditione;" the other Old Latin Mss. have "in siti et perditione." The error most likely crept in when a scribe accidentally transposed "siti" and "in", and then omitted "et" as superfluous.

In summarizing the study of the text of Reg. and Sang. 4, some question might arise if, in the light of their many readings unattested by Ms. 58 or by the other Greek, it is not likely that their text came from a Greek recension now altogether unknown. Such a possibility may exist, but it is more probable that their ultimate ancestor was made by an editor who, being unhampered by a demand for literal exactness, attempted only to make a readable narrative out of the story.

His source unquestionably was of the recension of which Ms. 58 probably is a more recent copy. That it was not Ms. 58 itself has been stressed in part, and will appear more clearly in the next section, where we shall see that a large number of the readings peculiar to 58 are not followed by Reg. and Sang. 4. It might easily have been, too, that the copy of the 58-recension, which he used, was lacking in places, and that wherever such was the case he filled in from whatever Mss. he had at hand, and it would seem, if this is the case, that the secondary source was akin to the text preserved in the uncial codices.

SANGERMANENSIS 15

This manuscript, which Sabatier says is "non minoris antiquitatis" than Reg. and Sang. 4, has a text practically as complete as theirs. The omissions of Sang. 15, as compared with the text of the uncial codices, are of a minor nature, being in no case as much as an entire verse. They are mostly phrases and clauses, and their number is relatively small. Neither does Sang. 15 add a great deal, and its additions, unattested by other versions, are not large in number. Consequently, in important particulars it presents the same account of Judith that the other important recensions have.

It is in its relationship to other manuscripts, however, that Sang. 15. becomes a very interesting version, and when one comes to investigate its family alliances, it is found to be an extremely significant manuscript from the critical point of view. The first thing that strikes one's attention is that it depends upon Ms. 58 in even a larger measure than Reg. and Sang. 4: e. g.,

9: 6. Uncials et al., ἡ κρίσις σου ἐν προγνώσει
Ms. 58, αἱ κτίσεις σου ἐν προγνώσει
Sang. 15, creatura tua in providentia
Reg. Sang. 4, judicia tua in providentia

Sang. 15 certainly got "creatura" from the reading of Ms. 58. In this instance, also, the reading of Reg. and Sang. 4, in not following 58, is noteworthy. The reading in the uncial text is the better one, and Reg. and Sang. 4 apparently chose the better text rather than follow the reading of Ms. 58.

5:11, Uncials et al., ἐτανείνωσεν αὐτούς
   Ms. 58, ἐταπείνωσεν τὸ πλῆθος αὐτῶν
   Sang. 15, humiliaverunt multitudinem eorum
   Reg. Sang. 4, humiliaverunt illos

The dependence of Sang. 15 upon Ms. 58 is again obvious, while the reading of Reg. and Sang. 4 again follows the uncial text.

15:7, Uncials, πεδινῇ ἐκράτησαν πολλῶν λαφύρων ἦν γὰφ πλῆθος πολὺ σφόδρα
   Ms. 58, πεδινῇ ἐκυρίευσαν πολλῶν λαφύρων
   Sang. 15, omnes campestres dominati sunt multorum praedam
   Reg. Sang. 4, multa spolia posederunt multitudo enim fuit magna

Sang. 15 does not literally reproduce the reading of Ms. 58, yet its use of "dominati sunt" and the omission of the last phrase of the uncial Greek show its dependence upon 58. Reg. and Sang. 4, on the other hand, have a reading that does not especially follow any Greek, although the clause, "multitudo enim fuit magna," establishes their relation to the uncial text.

11:22. Uncials, τοῦ γενηθῆναι ἐν χερσὶν ἡμῶν
   Ms. 58, τοῦ γενηθῆναι ἐν ἡμῶν
   Sang. 15, ut fiat in nobis
   Reg. Sang. 4, ut fiat in manibus nostris

In this instance, if there were but few like it, one would wonder if the omission of "manibus" were not an accident, but it is peculiar that Sang. 15 and Ms. 58 should omit the same word, and since just such omissions from both Mss. commonly occur (cf. also, 2:19; 6:13;

15:8; 15:11; 16:21) the possibility of the two being related becomes very certain.

8:13. Uncials,   καὶ οὐθὲν ἐπιγνώσεσθε
    Ms. 58,   καὶ οὐθεὶς γνώσεσθε
    Sang. 15,   et nemo intelligit
    Reg. Sang. 4,   quam nemo potest intelligere

Here again Sang. 15 very closely follows the reading of Ms. 58, while in Reg. and Sang. 4 there is another fine instance of their tendency toward free translation. The appearance of "quam," however, seems to show their alliance to the text of the uncials.

A long collection of illustrations can be brought forward further to illustrate the dependence of Sang. 15 upon Ms. 58; the number of the similarities is too great, and often their significance is too striking, to be lightly dismissed. And yet, as seen in the study of Reg. and Sang. 4,[1] there are a goodly number of cases when Sang. 15 does not agree with the variants of Ms. 58. However, if the relation of the text of Sang. 15 to Ms. 58 is compared with the relation existing between the text of Reg. and Sang. 4 and Ms. 58, one finds that Sang. 15 follows the variants of 58 much more frequently than do the other two. This fact is interesting and important, for with reference to the common judgment that the text of Ms. 58 is to be found in the Old Latin, one must point out in the first place that the variants of 58 are oftentimes overlooked by the "Old Latin;" and secondly, that the Old Latin Mss. do not in an equal degree adhere to the readings of Ms. 58.

Moreover, further study of Sang. 15 shows that this manuscript has affiliations with the text in Greek Mss. 19 and 108: e. g.,

1:4. Uncials et al.,   εἰς ὕψος πηχῶν ἑβδομήκοντα
        (Aleph, ἑξήκοντα)
    Mss. 19, 108,   εἰς ὕψος πηχῶν ὀγδομήκοντα
    Sang. 15,   in altitudine cubitorum octaginta
    Reg. Sang. 4,   in ·altum cubitiis sexaginta.

[1] Cf. above, pp. 14 ff.

Unquestionably, there must be a relation here between Sang. 15 and Mss. 19 and 108, in that both place the number of cubits at 80.

8: 9. Uncials et al., ἤκουσε
Mss. 19, 108, ἤκουσε 'Ιουδιθ
Sang. 15, audivit Judith
Reg. Sang. 4, audivit

11: 19. Uncials et al., κατὰ πρόγνωσίν μου
Mss. 19, 108, κατὰ πρόγνωσιν
Sang. 15, secundum providentiam
Reg. Sang. 4, secundum scientiam meam

Here again Sang. 15 attests the reading of Mss. 19 and 108, while the other Old Latin Mss. seem rather to read with the text of the uncial codices.

8: 8. Uncials et al., ἐπήγεγκεν αὐτῇ
Mss. 19, 108, ἐπήγεγκεν ἐπ' αὐτῇ
Sang. 15, diceret de ea
Reg. Sang. 4, inferret ei

In the word "diceret" there occurs a freedom of translation that Sang. 15 does not commonly show, and Reg. and Sang. 4 by the use of "inferret" adhere more closely to the Greek; but the whole phrase in Sang. 15 certainly shows the influence of Mss. 19 and 108, while "ei" in Reg. and Sang. 4 is from the uncial text.

Yet on the other hand, there are instances in which Sang. 15 does not follow the reading of Mss. 19 and 108: in 2: 19 these Mss. have 'Ολοφέρνης for αὐτὸς, and Sang. 15 has "ipse," but Reg. and Sang. 4 read "Olofernes;" again in 6: 4, Mss. 19 and 108 have τοῦ στόματος for τῶν λόγων, but Sang. 15 omits the expression altogether, while Reg. and Sang. 4 read "oris."[1] Once more, in 11: 9. Mss. 19 and 108 add the words πάντας τοὺς λόγους σου, which Sang. 15 fails to attest.[2] Consequently,

[1] In these few instances it appears that Reg. and Sang. 4 were contaminated by Mss. 19 and 108; the relationship should be noted, but there are few such instances all told, and none of importance.

[2] For other instances where the variants of Sang. 15 and Mss. 19 and 108 differ, see, 3: 3; 4: 9,10; 7: 27; 8: 10,21; 10: 3 &c.

the relation between Sang. 15 and Mss. 19 and 108 remains in doubt. Although, as seen, there are some instances in which the reading of Sang. 15 indubitably seems to have been influenced by the variants of Mss. 19 und 108, yet there are too many instances in which these relations do not exist. The most probable explanation of the situation seems to be that Sang. 15 depended largely on a manuscript of the recension of which 58 is a member, but that this manuscript was full of holes or had places where the readings could not be made out, as would be very common at the beginning or end of lines and with the top and bottom lines on pages, and in these places the translater used another text, which in some instances was of the type of Mss. 19 and 108, and in others the text of the uncial codices.

As to the relation of Sang. 15 to Reg. and Sang. 4, the difference between them in the examples cited above might seem to indicate that Sang. 15 was altogether independent of Reg. and Sang. 4. However, that there was some contamination between the two is certain, for there are numerous passages which show that the two texts must have been compared. To illustrate, in 7:18 Sang. 15 adds practically the came phrase to the text as Reg. and Sang. 4 do; Sang. 15 adds, "cum eis de plebe Assur duodecim milia," and the other two add, "cum eis plebis Assyriorum duodecim milia." This phrase is not attested by another Greek or Latin manuscript, so that the addition in both texts attracts one's attention. Of even more significance is the fact that these three Old Latin Mss. repeat the geneology of Judith in 8:7, after having given it in 8:1 as the rest of the recensions do. In 11:3, the three rather poorly translate εἰς τὸ λοιπὸν with the word, "deinceps." In 11:17, they translate μενῶ παράσοι, "manebo penes te;" in 15:8, for ἡ γερουσία they read "majores natu;" in 12:13, for βαγώας they have "Bagoas spado;" and in the next verse, "Bagoa spandone" for βαγώου. Now, it seems unlikely that Sang. 15 would have used "deinceps" in that sense, nor "penes" which is a rare translation of παρά, nor have added the word for eunuch in two instances, nor have translated γερουσία as "majores natu," without having felt the influence of the textual tradition of Reg. and Sang. 4.

On the other hand, the scribe of Sang. 15 was not slavishly dependent upon Reg. and Sang. 4, for wherever they give way to their habit of freedom of translation, Sang. 15 is inclined to produce a more literal translation, [1] e. g.

2: 27. Greek, θεσμοῦ πυρῶν
Reg. Sang. 4, triciti
Sang. 15, messis frumentium

The rendition of Reg. and Sang. 4 is indeed very free, apparently the translation of θεσμοῦ having dropped out, but in Sang. 15 we have a translation that follows the Greek closely.

7: 9. Greek, ἵνα μὴ γένηται θραῦσμα
Reg. Sang. 4, ne fiat in discussio
Sang. 15, ne fiat contractio

Again the independence of Sang. 15 is shown in this illustration, and in "contractio" we have a more literal translation of the Greek than in the phrase, "in discussio."

14: 20. Greek, ἰδὼν δέ
Reg. Sang. 4, postea veroquam vidit
Sang. 15, audiens autem,

Clearly in this case the reading of Sang. 15 is independent of Reg. and Sang. 4, and is a misreading of the Greek.

6: 4. Greek, νεκρῶν αὐτῶν
Reg. Sang. 4, mortuis
Sang. 15, cadaveribus eorum

The freedom of Reg. and Sang. 4 and the literal exactness of Sang. 15 sufficiently contrast to show the independence of the two texts.

5: 1 Greek, ἐτείχισαν πᾶσαν κορυφὴν ὄρους ὑψηλοῦ
Reg. Sang. 4, muri cinxerunt omnes vertices eorum
Sang. 15, munierunt omnes montes cacumen altissimi

Especially noticeable, here, is the expression in Reg. and Sang. 4, "muri cinxerunt," for ἐτείχισαν; whereas, Sang. 15 gives the literal equivalent, "munierunt." The

---

[2] Cf. also above, p. 18.

freedom of the text of the first two extends throughout the clause, and Sang. 15 clearly shows its independence.

1: 6. Greek, συνῆλθον ἔθνη πόλλα σφόδρα εἰς παράταξεν
Reg. Sang. 4, collegerunt se gentes multae ad bellum
Sang. 15, congretata sunt nationes multae valde ad pugnam

The fact that Sang. 15 differently translates the expression, παράχαξεν ἔθνη, and does not omit the translation of σφόδρα, shows that it is not dependent upon Reg. and Sang. 4 for its reading in this case.

13: 20. Greek, ἀπεξῆλθες πτώματι ἡμῶν ἐπ' εὐθείαν πορευθεῖσα
Reg. Sang. 4, prosilisti in casum ruinae nostrae in directum
Sang. 15, prospexisti in ruinam nostram per directum iens

In this example, again, Sang. 15 has abandoned the reading of Reg. and Sang. 4, setting forth what is awkward Greek in equally awkward Latin.

13: 20. Greek, ἐποιῆσαι σοι αὐτὰ ὁ θεὸς εἰς ὕψος αἰώνον
Reg. Sang. 4, det tibi Deus benedictionem in aeternus
Sang. 15, ut faciat tibi illa Deus in excelsis aeternus

Once more the freedom of Reg. and Sang. 4 is noteworthy, especially in that they specify the meaning of αὐτά by using "benedictionem;" Sang. 15 clearly avoids such freedom with the Greek and remains close to the literal meaning.

These instances have shown how Sang. 15 refuses to be guided by the text that is in Reg. and Sang. 4, especially in those instances when they are too free in the use of the material before them. But in a still further way the independence of Sang. 15 can be shown, by citing a few of the instances when it uses different words to express what seems certain to have been the same ground-text:

4:12, Greek, τοῦ μὴ δοῦναι εἰς διαρπαγὴν τὰ νήπια αὐτῶν
    Sang. 15, ne det in rapinam filios eorum
    Reg. Sang. 4, ut non daret in direptionem parvulos eorum

8:30. Greek, ἀπαγαγεῖν ὅρκον ἐφ' ἡμᾶς
    Sang. 15, aducere super nos juramentum
    Reg. Sang. 4, inducere super nos jusjurandum

In both of these citations the Latin texts undoubtedly came from the identical Greek, but the different prefix to the verbs and the different translations of the Greek word, ὅρκον, are noteworthy, for if Sang. 15 had depended on Reg. and Sang. 4 these differences would hardly have occurred.

7:17. Greek, παρενέβαλον ἐν τῷ αὐλῶνι
    Reg. Sang. 4, castra constituerunt in aulon
    Sang. 15, miserunt se in aulone

In this instance Sang. 15 does not render the Greek as faithfully as the other Mss. However, if it were a copy of Reg. and Sang. 4 such a reading would be unusual: rather the independence of Sang. 15 is again shown.

2:13. Greek, οὐ παραβήσῃ
    Reg. Sang. 4, non praeteries
    Sang. 15, non transgredieris

Sang. 15 has the more common equivalent for παραβήσῃ, but the other translation also is possible, and the probabilities are that the two translations were independently made.

4:5. Greek, πάσας τὰς κορυφὰς τῶν ὀρέων τῶν ὑψηλῶν
    Reg. Sang. 4, omnia cacumina montium excelsorum
    Sang. 15, omnes vertices montium altissimorum

The fact that Sang. 15 has "vertices" and "altissimorum" where Reg. and Sang. 15 respectively have "cacumina" and "excelsorum" shows its independence once more.

6:21. Greek,   ἐποίησε πότον τοῖς πρεσβυτέροις
Reg. Sang. 4,   fecit coenam senioribus
Sang. 15,   fecit epulum senioribus

It is possible that Sang. 15 considered "coenam" too weak for the Greek, πότον; "epulum" at any rate is a stronger term. But as with all these examples here we again have evidence that the editor who made Sang. 15 did not strictly depend upon the text of the older version.

Finally, passing mention should be made of the corruptions and misreadings in the text of Sang. 15. In 2:2, for the Greek, τὸ μυστήριον τῆς βουλῆς αὐτοῦ, "the secret of his counsel", Sang. 15 very peculiarly reads, "sacramentum regni sui." For one thing, this is indubitable proof that Sang. 15 was taken from the Greek rather than from the Hebrew, for the scribe apparently mistook or misread τὸ μυστήριον, and translated it in its theological sense. Also, he misread βουλῆς, and both of these errors could come from no other than a Greek source. In 5:2 where the Greek has τῆς παραλίας, Sang. 15, uses the peculiar word "parfalias," although in 5:22 Sang. 15 translates ταραλίας correctly. Consequently, in 5:2 apparently a local corruption caused him to misunderstand the word, and he therefore transliterated it. In 5:1, for σκάνδαλα, Sang. 15 has "tabernacula," and in 6:21, it reads "ecclesia" for τῆς ἐκκλησίας, another instance where the theological bias of the scribe seems to come to the fore. A considerable number of such illustrations could be added to this list to show the inferior quality of many of the variants of Sang. 15, and in this matter of corruptious the text of Sang. 15 has fared worse than Reg. and Sang. 4. However, by these variants this important fact receives additional confirmation: that Sang. 15 was an independent translation of the Greek.

For a summary of Sang. 15 this may be said: (1) it is an independent translation of the Greek, at least not a copy of any known manuscript of the Old Latin, and the text of Reg. and Sang. 4 in places has been used as a model: (2) its Greek source was the text of the recension of which Ms. 58 is a survivor, and perhaps where this text was uncertain, comparison was made with a text of the recension in the uncial codices, and in places with a text represented by the recension of Mss. 19 and 108; and (3) it is a translation of a later date than that represented by the ancestor of Reg. and Sang. 4; on the one hand, because of the fact that it is more slavish in its translations we have indication that it came from a later time, when the scribes were commencing to hold the text in higher reverence; and on the other, the peculiar type of corruptions of which it is guilty points to a greater lapse of time during which its sources had further opportunities of becoming contaminated.

PECHIANUS

In the introduction to Judith, Sabatier tells that this manuscript, considerably "decurtatus," was made for "D. D. Pech, S. Pauli Nabonensis Canonicus." Judging from its variant readings, one indeed cannot avoid agreeing that it must be a mutilated copy, for 159 of the 340 verses in the book of Judith are missing from Pechianus. In a large measure these omissions occur in gaps, in which a group of verses are lacking, so that in the manuscript many of the pages must have been damaged or torn out, as is shown by the fact, for example, that in the beginning of the manuscript the first chapter and three verses of the second are missing. However, oftentimes parts of verses are lacking, a phrase or a clause being gone, and consequently it seems likely that the text of Pechianus was abbreviated in the first place.

The most striking thing about Pechianus, even as Sabatier suggests, is its dependence upon Sang. 15. Of a long list of instances that can be brought forward, let us examine a few:

4:11. Greek,   ἐστωδώσαντο τὰς κεφαλάς
  Pech. Sang. 15, cinere capita sua impleverunt
  Reg. Sang. 4, cinerem posuerunt super capita sua
  Corbeiensis,   miserunt cinerem in capita sua

The relation between Pech. and Sang. 15, rather than between Pech. and any other V. L. Ms. is very obvious here, where there is considerable variation in the Old Latin.

6:4. Greek, ματαιωθήσεται
    Pech. Sang. 15, erunt inrita
    Other V. L., frustrabuntur

The different shade of meaning in "inrita" as against "frustrabuntur" is worthy of note, and the fact that Pech. and Sang. 15 alone have that reading further establishes their relation.

6:12. Greek, ἐπὶ τὴν κορυφὴν τοῦ ὄρους
    Pech. Sang. 15, ad verticem montis
    Reg. Sang. 15, super cacumen montis
    Corbeiensis, in frontem montis

The reading of Pech., "ad verticem," like Sang. 15, as against the reading of the other Mss. once more show their affiliations. The corruption in Corb. also is noteworthy.

6:17. Greek, ὅσα ἐμεγαλορρημόνησεν
    Pech. Sang. 15, omnia quaecumque magna superbe locutus est
    Reg. Sang. 4, quae magna locutus est
    Corbeiensis, quaecumque locutus est

This peculiar circumlocution in which Pech. and Sang. 15 concur adds a great deal of weight to their relationship, for such an expression could hardly be expected by accident

8:14. Greek, μηδαμῶς ἀδελφοὶ μὴ παρογίζετε
    Pech. Sang. 15, nolite fratres nolite errare et excerbare
    Reg. Sang. 4, nolite fratres nolite exacerbare

Here, the unattested words, "errare et," occurring only in Pech. and Sang. 15, again show their relation to each other.

14:5. Greek, πρὸ δὲ τοῦ ποιῆσαι ταῦτα
    Pech. Sang. 15, prius autem quam faciatis haec

14: 5. Reg. Sang. 4, et antequam faciatis ista
Corbeiensis, sed antequam faciatis haec

Here, Pech. and Sang. 15, besides producing a very literal translation are once more in verbal agreement. "Antequam" in the other Mss. is apparently a corruption of "autem quam."

14: 19. Greek, ὡς δὲ ἤκουσαν
Pech. Sang. 15, et factum est cum audissent
Reg. Sang. 4, quod cum audissent
Corbeiensis, et audierunt

The unattested appearance of "factum est" in Pech. and Sang. 15 is noteworthy, and yet since this expression begins a new section in the narrative the use of the phrase is perfectly natural. Still one's attention is called to the fact that these two alone read alike.

15: 2. Greek, μένων κατὰ πρόσωπον τοῦ πλησίον
Pech. Sang. 15, qui staret contra faciem proximi sui
Reg. Sang. 4, qui staret ante proximum suum
Corbeiensis, qui constaret contra faciem proximi sui

All the Old Latin Mss. attest the reading of a personal pronoun at the end of this clause, although no Greek Ms. has it, the difference between the Mss. is not great, but Pech. and Sang. 15 as against the rest literally agree.

14: 15. Greek, ὡς δὲ οὐδεὶς ἐπήκουσε διαστείλας
Sang. 15, et cum non audiretur post pussilum
Pech., et cum non audiretur intermissio spatio
Corbeiensis, et cum non audiret, aperuit
Reg. Sang. 4, postquam vero nullus respondebat, aperuit

In this instance the literal agreement between Pech. and Sang. 15 is not so close, although they do add the same idea. It would seem, therefore, that Pech. does not slavishly follow the variants of Sang. 15 in all instances.

From the instances cited above, however, it is fairly certain that in the first instance Pech. and Sang. 15 belong to the same family, for they alone have many peculiar readings which are unattested by other Old Latin manuscripts. Still it is equally evident that at times Pech. has been corrected from some other source. In the first place there is evidence that this correction was sometimes made from the recension of Reg. and Sang. 4; e. g.,

2:4. Greek, δεύτερον ὄντα μετ' αὐτὸν
Reg. Sang. 4, qui erat secundus ab eo
Sang, 15, secundo loco abs se
Pech. qui erat secundo loco post se

The reading of Pech., "secundo loco post se," clearly shows the influence of Sang. 15, and yet the reading "qui erat" seems to have been inspired by Reg. and Sang. 4. This phrase, however, might have fallen out of the text of Sang. 15 subsequently to the time of the writing of Pech.

15:4. Greek, τοὺς ἀπαγγέλλοντες ὑπὲρ τῶν συντετελεσμένων
Reg. Sang. 4, ut cognosceret de his rebus quae gesta erant
Sang. 15, qui nunciarent de consummatis
Pech. qui nuntiarent de rebus gestis

It seems almost certain that the phrase, "de rebus gestis," in Pech, was suggested by the reading of Reg. and Sang. 4, and yet the expression, "qui nuntiarent," seems likely to have been suggested by Sang. 15; so that most likely Pech. here has a conflate reading of the two recensions.

5:23. Greek, λαὸς ἐν ᾧ οὐκ ἔστι δύναμις οὐδὲ κράτος
Reg. Sang. 4, populos in quo non est potestas neque
Sang. 15, est multitudo in qua neque virtus una
Pech., est populus in quo neque virtus neque
εἰς παράταξιν ἰσχυράν
virtus in pugna valida
neque potestas est in pugna forte
potestas est in pugna

The thing to note here is that Pech. prefers the reading of Reg. and Sang. 4 in translating λαός, and omits the unattested word, "una;" which is in Sang. 15; otherwise its order is the same as in Sang. 15. This certainly looks as if in Pech. we have an attempt to improve the reading of Sang. 15 by using the other text.

16: 18. Greek, ἡνίκα ἐκαθαρίσθη (Mss. 19, 44, 71, 74, 76, 106, 236 add δέ after ἡνίκα)
Reg. Sang. 4, et postquam mundatus est
Sang. 15, mox autem purificatus est
Pech., et postquam purificatus est

Here is an obvious case in which Pech. has a conflate reading of the other two texts, having taken "et postquam" from Reg. and Sang. 4, and "purificatus est" from Sang. 15.

16: 25. Greek, οὐκ ἦν ἔτι ὁ ἐκφοβῶν
Reg. Sang. 4, non fuit adhuc qui in timore mitteret
Sang. 15, non erat iam qui perturbaret
Pech., non fuit ultra qui perturbaret

Again Pech. presents a conflate reading, "fuit" having come from Reg. and Sang. 4, while "qui perturbaret" shows the influence of Sang. 15 again.

On the other hand, Pech. seems also to have been corrected by comparison with the Greek; e. g.,

2: 5. Greek, ὁ βασιλεὺς ὁ μέγας ὁ κύριος πάσης τῆς γῆς
Reg. Sang. 4, rex magnus universae terrae Dominus
Sang. 15, rex magnus Dominus orbis terrae
Pech., rex magnus Dominus omnis terrae

Of course it is not possible to say whether the corruption in Sang. 15 of "orbis" for "omnis" occurred before Pech. was made or later; if it was later, Pech. very obviously corrected the corruption from the Greek.

14: 16. Greek, μετὰ κλαυθμοῦ καὶ στεναγμοῦ καὶ βοῆς ἰσχυρᾶς
Reg. Sang. 4, cum lacrymis et luctu
Sang. 15, cum fletu magno
Pech., cum fletu et gemitu et ulalato magno

The omission from Sang. 15, Pech. supplied from the Greek rather than from Reg. and Sang. 4.

15:3. Greek, τοτὲ οἱ υἱοί 'Ισραὴλ πᾶς ἀνὴρ πολεμιστὴς ἐξ αὐτῶν
  Reg. Sang. 4, tunc filiorum Israel omnis vir bellator
  Sang. 4, tunc filii Israel et omnis bellator eorum
  Pech., tunc filii Israel omnis vir bellator eorum

Two things in this instance show that Pech. likely was corrected from the Greek: no authority was found in the Greek for the word, "et," appearing in Sang. 15, so it was not retained; and the omission of "vir" was rectified. The Greek rather than Reg., and Sang. 4 has been used for reference, because if the latter had been used one would expect a different result.

5:20. Greek, ἐκπολεμήσομεν
  Reg. Sang. 4, expugnabimus
  Sang. 15, debellamus
  Pech. debellabimus

The correction of the tense of the verb used by Sang. 15, if indeed it is a conscious correction, certainly must have been suggested by the Greek.

12:16. Greek, καὶ ἦν κατεπίθυμος σφόδρα
  Reg. Sang. 4, quia erat cupiens valde
  Sang. 15, quia erat concupiscens valde
  Pech. et erat concupiscens valde

In general here again the relation between Pech. and Sang. 15 is obvious, but the fact that Pech. reads "et" for "quia" can be explained only by supposing that it was influenced by the Greek text.

14:13. Greek, καὶ παρεγένοντο
  Reg. Sang. 4, et venerunt
  Sang. 15, qui cum venissent
  Pech. qui cum convenissent

It seems very likely that in this instance Pech. took the prefix for its verb from the Greek.

5: 21. Greek,   οὐκ ἔστιν ἀνομία
Reg. Sang. 4, non est iniquitas
Sang. 15,   est justitia
Pech.,   non est injustitia

This exemple also is noteworthy, for it seems certain that Pech. used Sang. 15 as a source, but not liking the positive form in Sang. 15, followed the Greek, using the word "justitia," from Sang. 15, as a suggestion for the translation, "injustitia."

There are, of course, instances in which Pech. does not read with any of the Old Latin Mss., instances when corruptions have crept into te text: e. g., in 6: 3, for ῥύσεται it alone of the Old Latin has "defendet," a reading which the context may allow, but which certainly is unattested. In 10: 9, by a scribal error it has "ut eam," where all the rest of the Old Latin Mss. correctly read "ut exeam." In 4: 11, for ἀνήρ it reads "viventis," apparently a corruption of "juventis," the variant in Sang. 15. In 5 : 22, it translates συγκόψαι with the words, "interficere debere," and in 14: 5, in an equally peculiar way it translates ἀντιλαβέσθαι with the words, "ut opem feras." Rather a large number of similar corruptions exist, and indicate therefore that the manuscript was not done with too great care.

Concerning Pechianus, then, it seems probable that it belongs primarily to the recension of Sang. 15. It is equally probable that the scribe had other Mss. before him, and where the reading of Sang. 15 seemed doubtful or unsuitable he used one of these other texts for comparison. The text of Reg. and Sang. 4 and the Greek (apparently the uncial text) were the recensions thus referred to. This would make Pechianus the most recent version we have so far discussed.

CORBEIENSIS 7

Sabatier, in writing about this manuscript in his introduction to the Book of Esther, says that it is about 500 years old, that is, a manuscript of the 12th or 13th Century, and in the introduction to Judith he says that it is clearly written, howewer being from a late time.

As to the text in general, one of the first things one notices is the frequent omission of phrases and clauses. There are at least fifty verses in which part of the verse, often amounting to one-fourth or more, is lacking. These omissions are scattered through the entire book. For instance, taking the tenth chapter as a random illustration, of its 606 words 205 are missing; the chapter has twenty-three verses, and in the text of Corb. nine of them are partly lacking, the average amount being between one-fourth and one-third of the verse. In these nine cases we find only four attested by other Mss., one by the Vulgate, one by Ms. 106 and two by Ms. 71. In these omissions no particularly important material is left out, and the main movement of the narrative is kept up; so it would seem that these omissions are due to a determination on the part of the editor to put forth an abridged edition.

First, as to the relation between Corb. and the various Greek manuscripts, it is noteworthy that it agrees with the readings of Ms. 58 in only a few instances; e. g.,

5:14. Greek, εἰς ὁδὸν Σινά
    Ms. 58, εἰς ὄρος τὸ Σινά. (So also in some of the A—MSS)
    Corbeiensis, in monte Sina
    Other V. L., in viam Sina

The general knowledge of the scribe may have caused him to write "monte" instead of "viam;" still, the relation between Corb. and Ms. 58 is interesting.

13:14. Greek, αἰνεῖτε τὸν θεὸν αἰνεῖτε, αἰνεῖτε τὸν θεόν
    Ms. 58, αἰνεῖτε τὸν θεὸν ἡμῶν
    Corbeiensis laudate Deum nostrum
    Reg. Sang. 4, laudate Deum, laudate Dominum nostrum
    Sang. 15, Pech., laudate Deum nostrum laudate Deum

The text of the Greek very likely has been enlarged through dittography; still, most of the Old Latin Mss. attest that reading in some measure; but Corb. reads the same as Ms. 58.

4:6. Ms. 58 has Ἐλιακείμ where the rest of the Greek reads Ιωακίμ; Corb. and the Vulgate read, "Eliachim," and the other Old Latin Mss. have "Joachim." But here the Vulgate may have influenced the reading found in Corb.

The other instances in which Ms. 58 and Corb. seem to agree are in the omission of a word or a phrase (cf. 7:23; 7:22; 13:7). However, these instances are of relative unimportance, and since each of these two Mss. has a much longer list of omissions in which the other does not concur, the few agreements can not be given undue emphasis. As for the instances cited above, the second one only seems to be a clear case. For in the first, the variant may have come from one of the A-Mss. as well as from the reading of Ms. 58, and in the third case Corb. more likely got "Eliachim" from the Vulgate than from Ms. 58. So the instance in 13:14 is the only one in which a real comparison exists between the readings of Corb. and of Ms. 58, and yet the common habit of the editor of Corb. might have lead him to abbreviate his translation in a case where the Greek certainly has unnecessary repetition. One is inclined to take this attitude toward the relation existing between Corb. and Mss. 58, because Ms. 58 has a very long list of variants which Corb. does not attest,[1] and question therefore immediately arises about the few instances in which there seems to be a relation.

Practically the same can be said about the relation between Corb. and Mss. 19 and 108. A few passages seem to show a comparison:

10:3. Greek, $\mu\acute{\upsilon}\rho\omega$ $\pi\alpha\chi\epsilon\hat{\iota}$
Mss. 19 and 108, $\kappa\acute{\alpha}\lambda\omega$ $\pi\alpha\chi\epsilon\hat{\iota}$
Corbeiensis, ungento bono
Other V. L., ungento spisso
Vulgate, myro optimo

Here Corb. certainly gives the same reading as Mss. 19 and 108, and the Vulgate can hardly be considered an influence; although the fact that the Vulgate did not

---

[1] Cf. e. g., 2:2; 3:8; 5:2, 11; 6:5; 7:32; 8:9, 11; 10:20; 11:11, 18; 12:3, 7; 14:13; 15:5; 16:24 &c.

attest "spisso" might have been an influence to the scribe of Corb. to use "bono."

3:3.   Ms. 58 adds to the Greek,   πᾶς ἄργος
     Mss. 19 and 108 add,   πᾶς τόπος ἡμῶν
     Reg. and Sang. 4 read,   universus ager
     Corbeiensis reads,   omnis locus noster

Here again some of the Mss. of the A-group have the same variant as Mss. 19 and 108. However, Corb. reads with the Mss. of the A-group very rarely; so the facts are contradictory. At any rate, the reading of Corb. in this instance seems certain to have been suggested by one of these cursive groups, more probably by Mss. 19 and 108.

However uncertain may be the relation of Corb. to the various Mss., or groups of Mss., dealt with above, a much greater degree of certainty exists concerning the relation between Corb. and the Mss. of the B-group (i. e., Mss. 44, 71, 74, 76, 106, 107, 236). E. g.,

8:25.   Greek,   εὐχαριστήσωμεν κυρίῳ τῷ θεῷ ἡμῶν
     Mss. 44 and 106,   εὐχαριστήσωμεν τῷ θεῷ ἡμῶν
     Corbeiensis,   gratias agamus Deo noster
     Reg. Sang. 4 and 15,   gratias agamus et placeamus Deo nostro

In the first place, the reading of Reg. Sang. 4 and 15 is longer than the Greek, and the shortened reading of Corb. reproduces the variant of Mss. 44 and 106 rather than the standard Greek.

8:22.   Greek,   τῆς γῆς
     Mss. 44 and 106,   τῆς γῆς ἡμῶν
     Corbeiensis,   terrae nostrae
     Other V. L.,   terrae

9:3.   Greek,   θυγατέρας
     Mss. 44 and 106,   θυγατέρας αὐτῶν
     Corbeiensis,   filias eorum
     Other V. L.,   filias

13:11. Greek, κατὰ τῶν ἐχθῶν
Codex B, κατὰ τῶν ἐχθῶν ἡμῶν
Corbeiensis, de inimicis nostris
Other L. V., adversus inimicis

In these last few illustrations the additions to the text of Codex B or to the Mss. of the B-group have been attested by Corb. in each case. A few such might be dismissed, but they can be duplicated many times; e. g.,

2:27. Greek, ἀργοὺς αὐτῶν
Mss. 44 and 106, ἀργους
Corbeiensis, agros
Other Old Latin, agros illorum

7:1. Greek, πάσῃ τῇ στρατιᾷ αὐτοῦ
Mss. 44 and 106, πάσῃ τῇ στρατιᾷ
Corbeiensis, omni militae
Other Old Latin, omni militae suae

6:14. Greek, ἐπὶ τοὺς ἄρχοντας τῆς πόλεως αὐτῶν
Mss. 44 and 106, ἐπὶ τοὺς ἄρχοντας τῆς πόλεως
Corbeiensis, ad principes civitatis
Other Old Latin, ad principes civitatis suae

11:15. Greek, - δοθήσονται σοι εἰς ὄλεβρον
Mss. 44 and 106, δοθήσονται εἰς ὄλεβρον (also so in Ms. 55)
Corb.(Sang.15), dabuntur in perditionem
Reg. Sang. 4, dabuntur tibi in perditionem

These few citations illustrate a very characteristic relation between Corb. and Mss. of the B-group, especially Mss. 44 and 106, and it is especially with reference to the omissions that this similarity obtains.[1] However, these cursive Mss. make many omissions which Corb. does not attest; so it can not be stated that Corb. solely depended upon this textual tradition for its variant readings. The most likely explanation of the lack of agreement in all particulars is that these Mss. have been further corrupted subsequently to the time when Corb. or its ancestor, was written. Since the time, also, the ancestor of the cursive Mss., with which the recension in Corb. was

[1] Cf. also such variants as in 8:2; 10:6, 20; 11:1, 2, 3. 22; 14:5, 16.

compared, could easily have been corrupted in a further way; so that the transmission of the Greek cursive Mss., as well as the history of the immediate ancestors of Corb., may account for the lack of complete harmony between these two recensions. However, with reference to the wider relation between Corb. and the Greek, it seems, inasmuch as there are some instances where Corb. was contaminated by variants of Ms. 58 and of Mss. 19 and 108, and possibly by variants of the Mss. of the A-group, that its text is very composite, and that somewhere in its history it has suffered considerable contamination from a number of textual traditions.

Passing on to the relation between Corb. and the other Old Latin Mss., the instances already cited in the previous pages have pointed to the fact that there is little in common between them, for the readings of Corb. have almost continually varied from the rest of the Old Latin. And so it is as a matter of fact throughout the entire book; e. g.,

4:11. Greek, τὸ θυσιαστήριον σάκκῳ περιέβαλον
Reg. Sang. 4, cooperuerunt altare cilicio
Sang. 15, Pech., altare cilicio operuerunt
Corbeiensis, aram operuerunt cilicio

The appearance of the word, "aram," in the text of Corb. gives pretty clear evidence that Corb. is independent of the rest of the Old Latin.

15:3. Greek, οἱ παρεμβεβληκότες ἐν τῇ ὀρεινῇ
Reg. Sang. 4, qui castra collocaverunt
Sang. 15, Pech., qui posuerunt castra in montibus
Corbeiensis, qui extraicientes in montana

The word, "extraicientes," no doubt an error for "castra icientes," again shows that Corb. is unrelated to the other Old Latin Mss.

6:1. Greek, τοῦ δήμου ἀλλοφύλων
Corbeiensis, populi Allophylorum
Other V. L., populis alienigenarium

The transliterated word, "Allophylorum," shows that Corb. was taken from the Greek, and apparently no Old

Latin Mss. were at hand, at least none from which Corb. could get a translation of ἀλλοφύλων.

4:5. Greek, ὅτι προσφάτως ἦν τὰ πεδία αὐτῶν τεθερισμένα
Corbeiensis, quia rescindentes campum illorum erant demensi
Other V. L., quia nuper erant campi eorum demessi

Once more, if Corb. were dependent on one of the Old Latin Mss., it would not have made the mistake of having "rescindentes" for "nuper erant."

7:3. Greek, παρενέβαλον ἐν τῷ αὐλῶνι πλησίον
Corbeiensis, commiserunt ad populum cura
Reg. Sang. 4, applicuerunt se in aulonam secus
Sang. 15, miserunt se in aulone justa

The peculiar mistranslation of which Corb. is here guilty again shows that it is independent of the other Old Latin versions.

13:2. Greek, ὑπελείφθη δὲ Ιουδὶθ μόνη
Corbeiensis, et erat Judith sola
Other V. L., derelecta est autem sola Judith

Here it almost seems that Corb. depended upon a source entirely different from anything we have, but at any rate it is clear that the other Old Latin versions did not affect it.

So then, as to the relation between Corb. and the other Old Latin Mss.[1] the evidence points very clearly to the fact that Corb. represents a different recension altogether. On the whole its deviation from the standard Greek is not great enough to suppose that its Greek source also was an unknown recension, although it does have a considerable number of variants that are unattested. However, its relation to the cursive Mss. of the B-group, and especially to Mss. 44 and 106, is sufficient to suppose that its Greek source was some manuscript out of this recension, and that it is a new translation of this source independent of all the rest of the Old

[1] Cf. also, 1:10; 2:13; 3:2, 10; 7:3, 6; 8:29; 10:8: 12:6; 16:23.

Latin, at least independent of those Old Latin recensions that still survive.

Finally, it must be emphasized that, although Corb. may be independent of the Old Latin, it shows unmistakable traces of having been compared with the Vulgate. The other Old Latin Mss. have shown no sign of such a comparison, but in Corb. evidence can be found in almost every verse. To illustrate:

3:8. Greek,   τὰ ἄλση αὐτῶν ἐξέκοψε
    Sang. 15,   templa eorum excidit
    Corbeiensis,   excidit lucos eorum
    Vulgate,   lucos eorum excidit

Although "lucos" is a better translation of the Greek than "templa," still it is noteworthy that Corb. and the Vulgate read alike (the other V. L. Mss. have omitted the expression).

5:19. Greek,   οὗ διεσπάρησαν ἐκεῖ (Mss. 44 and 106 omit ἐκεῖ)
    Reg. Sang. 4,   qua dispersi sunt ibi
    Corb., Vulg.,   qua dispersi fuerunt

Here apparently the reading of Mss. 44 and 106 seems to have been influential in the omission of "ibi," but also the tense of the verb establishes a connection between Corb. and the Vulgate.

8:4. Greek,   μῆνας τέσσαρας
    Other V. L.,   mensibus quatuor
    Corb., Vulg.,   mensibus sex.

The fact that Corb. and the Vulgate alone read, "sex," makes it probable that they are related.

8:23. Greek,   μετὰ τῆς ἄβρα μου καὶ ἐν ταῖς ἡμέραις
    Other V. L.,   cum ancilla me et in diebus
    Corbeiensis,   cum abra mea in diebus enim quinque
    Vulgate,   cum abra mea in diebus   quinque

The peculiar word, "abra," unknown to the Latin, and a transliteration of the Greek makes it very probable once more that Corb. and the Vulgate have been compared, as the addition of the word, "quinque" also shows.

11:12. Greek, ἐπιβαλεῖν τοῖς κτήνεσιν
Other V. L., injicere manus jumentis
Corbeiensis, interficere pecora
Vulgate, ut interficiant pecora

The appearance of "pecora" in both Corb. and the Vulgate indicates their connection, and the use of the same verb, although they use different forms of "interficio," also adds to the likelihood of their being related.

12:13. Greek, μὴ ὀρνήσατο δὴ ἡ παιδίσκη ἡ καλὴ αὕτη
Other V. L., non pigeat puellam bonam
Corb., Vulg., non revereatur bona puella

14:6. Greek, ἐξελύθη τὸ πνεῦμα αὐτοῦ
Other V. L., resolutus est spiritus eius
Corb., Vulg., aestuavit anima eius

16:19. Greek, εἰς ἀνάθημα τῷ θεῷ ἔδωκε
Reg. Sang. 4, dedit in consecrationem Domino
Corbeiensis, in oblivium anathema
Vulgate, in anathema oblivionis

In each of these last three instances the relation between Corb. and the Vulgate is so apparent that there can be no doubt about their having influenced each other. In the following passages it is perhaps possible to see on which side the comparing was done.

6:15. Greek, Ἀβρις ὁ τοῦ Γοθονιὴλ καὶ Χαρμὶς υἱὸς Μελχιήλ
Other V. L., Chabris filius Gothoniel et Charmis filius Melchiel
Corbeiensis, Carmi qui et Gothoniel et Charu filius Machiel
Vulgate, Charmi qui et Gothoniel

Here, if the Vulgate were dependent on Corb. then the omission of the last phrase would be unintelligible, for St. Jerome rarely makes such omissions when his source is clear. But, rather, Corb. accepted the testimony of the Vulgate as against the Greek that Gothoniel was the son of Charmi, i, e., Χαρμίς, and then added the last clause according to his Greek source, avoiding, however, the double use of the name, "Charmis," hence the corrupt, "Charu."

12: 16. Greek, ἐξέστη ἡ καρδία Ὀλοφερνοῦ ἐπ' αὐτῶν καὶ ἐσαλεύθη ἡ ψυχή
      Other V. L., expavit cor Olofernes in ea et commota est anima
      Corbeiensis, concussum est cor Olofernes in ea et commota est anima
      Vulgate, cor autem Holofernes concussum est

Again, if the Vulgate were dependent upon Corb. one would not expect to find it omitting the last clause, but rather Corb. more probably depended upon its Greek source, taking the suggestion, "concussum est," from the Vulgate.

13: 15. Greek, ἀρχιστρατήγου δυνάμεως
      Reg. Sang. 4 and 15, principis virtutis
      Corbeiensis, principis militae virtutis
      Vulgate, principis militae

Here Corb. gives itself away, for its reading is clearly a conflate of the Greek and the Vulgate. So that it would seem that Corb. had been contaminated by the Vulgate, rather than the contrary being true.

In summarizing the relationships of the Corbeiensis manuscript, then, several facts should be noted: (1) it seems to be an independent translation of the Greek, in which the readings of several Greek recensions appear, but among which the recension of the B-Mss. seems to be the dominant text; (2) it is a considerably abbreviated recension; (3) it is independent of any Old Latin Mss. known at the present time; and (4) it has been compared with the Vulgate in an extensive fashion, in this respect being unique in that it is the only Old Latin version which shows the influence of the Vulgate.

SUMMARY OF THE OLD LATIN

The Old Latin manuscripts of Judith fall into three recensions, Reg. and Sang. 4 forming one, Sang. 15 and Pech. belonging to the second, and Corb. being the third. These three recensions are largely independent. Although there is evidence of some contamination between the first and second, they nevertheless are sufficiently different to make it necessary to suppose that they represent two distinct translations. The third, the recension of Corbeiensis, seems to have been entirely independent of the other two, and has a special charateristic, which the others lack, in being rather extensively compared with the Vulgate. There is indubitable evidence that all three recensions were made from the Greek; the first depended largely on a text akin to the recension found in cursive Ms. 58, which it rendered with some degree of freedom; the second, exercising greater care in the matter of literal exactness, depended to a larger extent on Ms. 58, with some corruptions from the text of Mss. 19 and 108; and the third, critically the least dependable, is a mixed text in which the Uncials and the variants of the B-Mss. figured mostly, with contaminations from some of the other Greek recensions and from the Vulgate.

This being the case, it is necessary to point out once more that such a term as "Old Latin Version" must be used with greater care than heretofore, for in Judith there are at least *three* "Old Latin" versions, and their family differences are of such critical importance that in future textual studies, in which the Old Latin plays a part, it will be as important as it has become in the case of the Greek to distinguish between these recensions.

III
THE VULGATE

St. Jerome writes as follows in his preface to the Book of Judith: "Liber Judith inter Hagiographa legitur ... Chaldaeo sermone conscriptus inter historias computatur. Sed quia hunc librum Synodus Nicaena in numero Sanctarum Scripturarum legitur computisse, acquievi postulatione vestrae, imo exactioni, et sepositis occupationibus quibus vehementur arcetabar, huic unam lucubratiunculum dedi, magis sensum e sensu quam ex verbo verbum transferens. Multorum codicum varietatem vitiosissimam amputavi; sola ea, quae intelligentia integra in verbis Chaldaeis invenire potui, Latinis expressi." It would appear, then, that from the large number of defective manuscripts in existence in his time he selected an Aramaic document for the source of the translation now to be found in the Vulgate. Indirectly, this statement adds confirmation to Origen's remark, already referred to, that the Book of Judith did not exist in the Hebrew Apocrypha, for if the Hebrew original had been in existence, Jerome would certainly have used it in preference to a later version.

From the negative point of view, we can say with a fairly good degree of assurance that Jerome did not make his translation from the Greek, and in so far it may be probable that he did make it from the "Chaldee." A superficial comparison between the Vulgate and the Greek shows that the common judgment that there was no relation between them is unquestionably correct. For, of the 340 verses in the Greek text the Vulgate omits 42 entirely and large parts of 45 more. In the remaining verses the Vulgate agrees with the Greek more or less closely only about one half of the time, and literally reproduces the material in the Greek in relatively few instances. As for the rest of the book, about one-third in amount, the same trend of narrative can be recognized, sometimes abbreviated (as in 7: 23; 8: 9 f.; 9: 14; 11: 13; &c.), and sometimes expanded (as in 6: 21; 6: 3; 8: 34; &c.), but on the whole the method of expression and the order of the words is so completely changed in the Vulgate that it is hard to believe that it came from the Greek. For example, in the introductory verses of the book one may find a very typical instance of the way in which the Vulgate commonly compares with the Greek:

Ἔτους δωδεκάτου τῆς βασιλείας	
Ναβουχοδονοσόρ, ὃς ἐβασίλευσεν	
ἐν Νινευῆ τῆ πόλει τῆ μεγάλῃ	[orum,
ἐν ταῖς ἡμέραις Ἀρφαξάδ, ὃς	Arphaxad itaque, rex Medi-
ἐβασίλευσεν Μήδων ἐν Ἐκβατάνοις	subjugaverunt multas gentes
καὶ ᾠκοδόμησεν ἐπ᾽ Ἐκβατάνων	imperio suo, et ipse aedificavit
καὶ κύκλῳ τείχη ἐκ λίθων	civitatem potentissimam, quam
λελαξευμένων, εἰς πλάτος	appellavit Ecbatanis, ex
πηχῶν τριῶν καὶ εἰς μῆκος	lapidibus quadratis et fectis,
πηχῶν ἕξ, καὶ ἐποίησεν τὸ ὕψος*	fecit muros eius in latitudinem
τοῦ τείχους πηχῶν ἑβδομήκοντα,	cubitorum septuaginta,
καὶ τὸ πλάτος αὐτοῦ	et in altitudinem
πηχῶν πεντήκοντα	cubitorum triginti.

(* Codex A reads, μῆκος)

Finally in the fifth verse of the first chapter the Vulgate inserts what it omitted in the first; the narrative goes on as follows:

καὶ ἐποίησεν πόλεμον	Anno igitur duodecimo regni sui
ἐν ταῖς ἡμέραις ὁ βασιλεὺς	Nabuchodonossor rex Assyriorum,
Ναβουχοδονοσὸρ πρὸς βασιλέα	qui regnabat in Ninive civitate
Ἀρφαξάδ ἐν τῷ πεδίῳ τῷ με-	magna, pugnavit contra Arphaxad
γάλῳ τοῦτό ἐστιν ἐν τοῖς	et obtinuit eum in campo magno
ὁρίοις Ῥαγαῦ.	qui appellatur Ragau.

Now of course, the transposition of the first couple of lines of the book to a later verse is in itself no great novelty, and if that were all, not much could be said; but the entire structure of the introduction has been made over, and although the same general idea obtains, still almost every detail is in some way changed, so that it is almost a certainty that the Latin before us was not taken from this Greek.

Furthermore, the Vulgate adds 32 verses (e. g., 4: 12—14; 5: 15—19; 6: 16—18; 7: 19—22; 8: 24f.; 9: 7—9; 14: 9f. &c.), which are unattested by Greek or Latin. This material as a matter of fact adds nothing new in sense, but merely enlarges on the topic under discussion. However, in these passages one frequently finds Semitic idioms so baldly translated that is seems certain that they were rendered direct from a Semitic text; for when one finds such unmistakable Semitic expressions in the additions it is likely that they come from a source which was Semitic. E. g.,

2: 26. Here the Vulgate has the expression, "occidit in ore gladii," and in 15: 6, "persecuti sunt eos in ore gladii." The expression, "in (i. e., with) the mouth of the sword." is unmistakable, and literally translates what a Semitic document would have.

5: 20 (5: 24). The Vulgate has, "quoniam tradens tradet illos Deos eorum tibi et subjugati erunt sub jugo potentiae tuae." Especially the words, "tradens tradet," attract attention, since they represent a very common idiom used in a number of the Semitic languages.

5: 18 (5: 22). The Vulgate reads, "cum recessissent a via quam dederat illis Deus ut ambularent in ea." Two things are to be noted here: the common Semitic word order in "quam dederat illis Deus," having the verb and pronominal suffix precede the subject; and the idiom, "quam .... in ea," in which we have a literal translation of the word order which several Semitic languages use in order to express, "in which."

Likewise in other places (see also 9: 14; 1: 7; 8: 26; 4: 3; 5: 14) one may find expressions which have such an unmistakable tone of the Semitic that one is forced to the conclusion that they were taken directly from a Semitic document, and certainly not from the Greek.

So, because of the many differences that are to be noted between the Vulgate and the Greek, differences in the amount of the text and in the manner of expression, and because of the peculiar type of idiom which occurs with frequency throughout the Vulgate, the possibility of the Vulgate having been taken from the Greek can be dismissed as very unlikely. Then, if we may believe Jerome, the source was an Aramaic manuscript.

However, with reference to this source of the Vulgate, the common judgment since Fritzsche's time has been that Jerome produced a hasty and abridged paraphrase of the Old Latin. But if this contention is true, then the additions, just referred to, were added by him arbitrarily. But Jerome, when he is not translating, always uses a very idiomatic Latin; why then, would he in these instances, when he had no source to depend upon, fall into the use of such atrocious Latin as has lately been pointed out? On the contrary, is it not more likely that he was rendering the Aramaic version, which itself had these additions and in which such idioms would appear? This material—"Homeletical additions," Professor Porter defines it[1]—is of the character one should expect in an Aramaic version written for circulation among the later Jews. and reminds one of the Aramaic Targums with its pious references to the history of the race and to the religious customs of the Jews. Now, since there is no reliable evidence that Jerome depended upon the Old Latin, it might be well to consider with genuine seriousness his statement that he depended upon the "Chaldee" despite the fact that there has been a tendency in recent years to discredit St. Jerome at every point.[2]

[1] For a complete discussion of the character of these additions, see, F. C. Porter, art. on *Judith*, Hasting's, *Dictionary of the Bible*, Vol. II, pp. 822—824.
[2] A lengthy discussion on the inaccuracies of St. Jerome may be found in a monogram by Alfred Schmidtke, *Neue Fragmente und Untersuchungen*, in Harnack & Schmidt, *Texte und Untersuchungen*, Vol. 37, pp. 253 ff.

Moreover, with reference to this judgment that the Vulgate is a paraphrase of the Old Latin, in the discussion of the Old Latin Mss. it was shown that Corbeiensis alone was affiliated with the Vulgate, and that it is dependent on the Vulgate rather than vice versa. To this general statement, that only Corb. is related to the Vulgate there is one exception, which occurs in Judith's hymn of praise (16: 2—17), and it is this passage in which Cowley finds his principal reasons for supposing the Vulgate to be related to the Old Latin.[1] In these verses Corb. has almost no affiliations with the Vulgate, while Reg. and Sang. 4 frequently attest the variants of the Vulgate, E. g.

In 16: 2 Reg. and Sang. 4 agree with the Vulgate in rendering ἐναρμόσασθε as "modolamini," Sang. 15 has "cantate," and Corb., "facite." In 16: 5 they have "incensurum se" for ἐμπρήσειν, and later in the verse they have "occisurum" for ἀναλεῖν; in the respective places Sang. 15 has "succendere" and "occidere," and Corb. has "ut incederet" and "ut interficeret." In 16: 10 The Vulgate and Reg. and Sang. 4 again agree in reading "constantiam" for τὴν τόλμαν, while Sang. 15 and Corb. read "audaciam." In 16: 12, for κατεκέντησαν the three have "compunxerunt," while Sang. 15 and Corb. read "interfecerunt." In nearly every verse of the Song some such similarity may be pointed out between the Vulgate and Reg. and Sang. 4, while the similarities between the Vulgate and Corb. are very small in number and never of a striking nature.[2]

At first one might be inclined to think that in this passage the text of the Vulgate and that of Reg. and Sang. 4 had been compared, but a closer examination of the variant readings of these two recensions shows that such is not the case. There are as many instances, practically speaking, in which the Vulgate fails to attest the readings of Reg. and Sang. 4 as when it does. To illustrate, in 16: 3, for ἐκ χειρός τῶν

---

[1] A. E. Cowley, in Charles' *Apogrypha and Pseudepigrapha of the O. T.*, Vol. I, p. 244.

[1] The variants of Corb. and the Vulgate seem to agree only in 16: 4; 7; 15; 17.

καταδιωκόντων με the Vulgate reads, "de manu omnium inimicorum nostrorum," while the other two read, "de manibus persequentium me." In 16:4, for ἐν μυριάσι δυνάμεως αὐτοῦ the Vulgate reads, "in multitudine fortitudinis suae," Reg. and Sang. 4 read, "in millibus exercitus sui," and Corb., "in millia virtutum suarum." In 16:5, for σκυλεῦσαι Reg. and Sang. 4 have "spoliaturum," the Vulgate reads "in captivitatem," so also Sang. 15, and Corb. has "in praeda." Finally, one more illustration from 16:9:

Greek, διῆλθεν ὁ ἀκινάκης τὸν τράχηλον αὐτοῦ
Reg. Sang. 4, amputavit pugione cervicem eius
Vulgate, amputavit gladius caput eius
Sang. 15, divisit pugio cervicem illus
Corbeiensis, transivit gladius cervicem eius

This instance makes it hard to see how the Vulgate could have been influenced by the Old Latin. To hold such a conclusion would be a confusing process; one would have to say that it got "amputavit" from the recension of Reg. and Sang. 4, "gladius" from Corb., a different recension, and finally, that "caput" was taken from an altogether different source, or that Jerome himself was responsible for that variation. The fact of the matter is that Jerome's translation of the Song is probably an independent one. A song or psalm, or any bit of poetry for that matter, is less likely to suffer corruption in the process of transmission than plain narrative; partly because of the fact that its metrical and rhythmic elements will longer adhere to memory, and also because it is usually expressed in such terse phraseology that a great deal of variation is impossible. Consequently, the part of the book of Judith that would be most constant would no doubt be this very section, and hence Jerome in translating his source could very conceivably have many points in common with these other translations, without necessarily having depended upon them. So although there are some interesting comparisons between the Vulgate and the text of Reg. and Sang. 4, still there are just as many instances, equally striking, in which their readings do not correspond; as a result it is hardly probable that from this short poem one can obtain much evidence to support the contention that the Vulgate was dependent upon the Old Latin.

Aside from the general considerations already pointed out, that the Vulgate comes from a Semitic source, there is concrete evidence that this Semitic source was Aramaic. In the Aramaic one of the most constant features is the use of the particle די. In a translation the occurrence of this word will often escape notice, especially where it expresses the genitive relationship, and oft times where it stands as a relative pronoun. But in the other places, where it stands as a particle introducing a subordinate clause, what Latin particle would be likely to stand in its place? Would it not in all probability be "ut?" Now it happens that in the Vulgate the particle "ut" is much more commonly used than in the Old Latin. It appears in the Vulgate at least 70 times, and in the same passages the Old Latin uses "ut" but 15 times, although of course in other places the Old Latin makes some use of the ut-clause, but not nearly such common use as the Vulgate. In every case where the Vulgate makes use of this particle, it stands where one would find the Aramaic די; to illustrate.

- 3:2. "Melius est enim ut viventes serviamus..." (The Vulgate has the same expression in 7:16 also). In this case there can be no doubt but that the Aramaic particle would be back of "ut."
- 6:2. "Quod gens Israel defendatur a Deo suo, ut ostendam tibi..." Not only the use of "ut," but also that of "quod" should be noted. Both stand in representative places of די. Likewise in 8:10, "quod est hoc verbum... ut tradat," both "quod" and "ut" stand together in a similar relation.
- 15:7. "Mox autem ut ortus est dies..." and also in 16:22, "et mox ut purificati sunt," and again in 6:5, "ut autem noveris quia..." In all these instances the use of "ut" would hardly be expected in good Latin, although it very appropriately stands for the Aramaic particle.

Then, too, the words "ita ut" rather commonly appear in the Vulgate. These words are the logical expression of the

Aramaic word, כְּדִי. Their occurrence for the most part takes place where one would expect to see this Aramaic expression; e. g., 15:2, "ita ut nullus loqueretur;" 10:13, "ostendam illi... ita ut non cadat vir;" 7:11, "defecerunt cisternae... ita ut non esset;" 5:12. "Deus coeli mare aperuit, ita ut..." (cf. also, 4:16; 6:18; 13:28; 15:8; 16:16.) In all of these instances the use of this expression corresponds exactly with the usage of the Aramaic idiom; and the fact that St. Jerome uses this expression more frequently than it appears in the Old Latin argues that he most probably had a source in which that kind of expression was more common. And the source in which it would be most common would be an Aramaic source; consequently the internal evidence of the Vulgate indicates that we may accept Jerome's statement that he translated a "Chaldee" document.

Furthermore, if an examination is made of the proper names appearing in the Vulgate, one comes upon some corruptions of an interesting nature. In 1:6, the Vulgate reads "Jadason" for $Y\delta\acute{a}\sigma\pi\eta\nu$; Reg., Sang. 4 and Corb. read "Udaspia," and Sang. 15 reads "Hydnas." Obviously the reading in the Vulgate is a corruption of the Greek, but the mistake was more likely made by the scribe of the Aramaic than by Jerome, for he is generally very careful about proper names, and it is much more probable that he got "Jadason" form a corrupt Aramaic word than from the Greek. However, this intermediate source, the Aramaic, unquestionably is derived from the Greek. Again in 1:9, for $\Gamma\acute{\epsilon}\sigma\epsilon\mu$ the Vulgate reads "Jesse," and the Old Latin Mss. read with the Greek. One wonders why Jerome failed to recognize "Goshen," and he certainly would have recognized it if he had had the Old Latin or the ordinary Greek text before him. So again, one is inclined to feel that the corruption was in Jerome's source, in which the final letter, "Nûn," could easily have dropped out. Once more, in 8:1, for $'\Omega\xi$ the Vulgate reads "Idox;" Reg. and Sang. 4 have "Ozi;" Sang. 15 reads "Jacob;" and Corb., again showing the influence of the Vulgate, reads "Idox." Very obviously in this instance the reading of the Vulgate again comes from the Greek in the last analysis, rather than from the typical Old Latin Mss. Reg., Sang. 4, and 15; for the corruption, "Idox," could hardly be expected from "Ozi" or "Jacob."

Consequently, in these corrupt proper names we have further evidence of a very convincing nature that the Vulgate was independent of the Old Latin. It also is apparent that the *source* of the Vulgate was independent of the Old Latin, but was related to the Greek as these proper names show. It would seem, then, that the Aramaic version, upon which St. Jerome depended, was itself a translation of a Greek version considerably different from the Greek versions now extant.

BIBLIOGRAPHY

The following studies make up a partial bibliography on the Book of Judith, being the works in which especially the text and the relations among the versions are discussed:

Fabricius, M. Joh. Albertus, *Liber Tobae, Judith, Oratio Manassae, Sapientia, et Ecclesiasticus.* (Leipzig 1691.)

Fritzsche, O. F., *Das Buch Judith*, in the *Exegetisches Handbuch zu den Apokryphen des Alten Testamentes.* (Leipzig 1858.)

Ball, C. J., *Judith*, in the *Speakers Commentary.* (London 1888.)

Zöckler, O., *Judith*, in *Die Apokryphen des Alten Testamentes.* (Munich 1891.)

Lohr, Max, *Judith*, in *Die Apokryphen des Alten Testamentes.* Edited by Kautzsch. (Tübingen 1900.)

Cowley, A. E., *The Book of Judith*, in Charles' *Apocrypha and Pseudepigrapha of the Old Testament.* Vol. I. (Oxford 1913.)

Porter, F. C., Article entitled, *Judith*, in Hastings, *Dictionary of the Bible.*

Schürer, Emil, *The History of the Jewish People in the Time of Jesus Christ*, II, iii. pp. 32 ff.

www.ingramcontent.com/pod-product-compliance
Lightning Source LLC
Chambersburg PA
CBHW071800040426
42446CB00012B/2648